KU-512-017

TABLE OF CONTENTS

1

What do you picture when you think of a rock? Ask a climber, and he or she will say a mountain. Ask a jeweler, and he or she will say a diamond ring. Ask a scientist, and he or she will say our planet, sometimes called the third rock from the sun. The more you know about minerals, rocks, **geodes**, and gems—what are they, how are they alike, and how are they different—the more you'll know about our planet.

MINERALS

Let's start with **minerals**, the building blocks of rocks and gems. Minerals are made of **atoms** arranged in a **uniform** pattern.

Crystal Clear

Because of the way they're formed, most minerals are crystals, like a grain of salt that you would shake on your french fries. Salt is just one mineral you eat. Your body needs various minerals to stay healthy.

FLUORITE

ROCKS

Rocks are made of two or more minerals. But unlike minerals, they can contain material from living things. Earth's surface is made of rock.

MINERALS, ROCKS, GEODES, AND GEMS

GEODES

From the outside, geodes look like hardened lumps of dough. But don't be fooled, because inside they contain rainbow hues of beautiful crystals, making geodes a stunning combination of rocks, minerals, and gems.

GEMS

Gems are minerals that have been cut and polished to make them pretty. Of the more than 4,000 minerals in the world, fewer than 100 are used to make gems. Diamonds—classified as mineral, gem, and crystal—are among the hardest materials on Earth.

Minerals are the building blocks of rocks and gems.

In the same way that your fingerprints make you unique, minerals have special features, called properties, that make them different from one another. Take a look at the box on the next page to learn more about these six properties.

ROCK-HARD FACT

A mineral's properties come from the inside out, based upon its **composition** and how its atoms are arranged.

About a third of the water we drink comes from rocks underground. Minerals from rocks strengthen our bodies and help water taste better.

ARTESIAN WELL

SOIL

LOAM
SAND AND GRAVEL
WATER

LOAM

CLAY

IMPERMEABLE ROCK
(LIMESTONE)

WATER

MINERALS

PYRITE, AKA "FOOL'S GOLD"

6 PROPERTIES OF MINERALS

1. **Specific gravity:** How heavy is it compared to the same amount of water?

2. **Luster:** Is it shiny or dull?

3. **Transparency:** Can you shine a flashlight through it?

4. **Hardness:** How hard is it? Can you scratch it with your fingernail, or could it scratch you—or even glass?

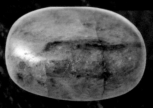

5. **Color:** What color is it? Some minerals, such as beryl, can come in different colors.

EMERALD BERYL

AQUAMARINE BERYL

6. **Streak:** When you rub it across a rough surface, what color streak does it make? The streak test shows the mineral's true color.

MYSTERIOUS MAGNETITE

It was spring 2008 in Sichuan, China. Toads littered the streets. At the local zoo, zebras banged their heads. Elephants, lions, and tigers paced, stomped, and growled. Peacocks screeched. Then a deadly magnitude 8 earthquake shook the region.

Scientists believe that the animals' behavior was a result of their sensing the coming disaster. How? Well, scientists think magnetite, which is found in animals' brains, helped them sense changes in Earth's **electromagnetic** field. The changes might have given the animals headaches that affected their behavior.

Earthquake in Sichuan, China, 2008

MAGNETITE

ROCK-HARD FACT

The ability of living things to sense magnetic fields is called **magnetoreception,** which gives animals a kind of mental map to help them find where they're going.

STRANGE-BUT-TRUE STORIES

A FINE FIND IN FELDSPAR

For a long time, the process of making porcelain—the material used to make the china dishes you're never allowed to touch at your grandma's house—was a secret known only to the Chinese. But in 1710, Johann Frederick Bottger, a prisoner of Germany's King Augustus discovered that secret: ground-up feldspar, a common mineral.

This was a very valuable secret since no one in Europe knew how to make porcelain, or "white gold" as it was known then. King Augustus jumped on the chance to become very wealthy by holding Bottger as his prisoner while he made one porcelain dish after another. The king finally set Bottger free after twelve years.

ROCK-HARD FACT

About 60 percent of the rocks in Earth's crust are made of a type of feldspar. The mineral is also used in glassmaking, ceramics, paint, plastic, and rubber.

Feldspar as Fine Porcelain

Minerals, which are always solid, are made when magma melts and cools beneath Earth's surface. As a result, water **evaporates**, leaving behind crystals of minerals. (Remember our grain of salt?) When magma cools quickly, small mineral crystals result. When it cools slowly, larger mineral crystals result.

Mineral Crystals under a Microscope

Most mineral crystals are so tiny that you can only see them under a microscope. But some, such as gypsum crystals found in caves around the world, are larger than life!

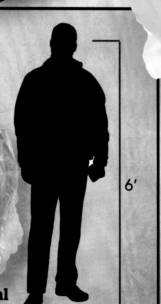

Quartz Crystal

6'

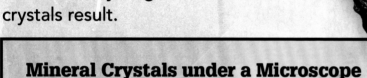

A MINEFIELD OF MINERAL FACTS

CALCOPYRITE

Spodumene: Take a Second Look—and a Third!

When you look at the mineral spodumene, you may think your eyes are playing tricks on you—and for good reason. The mineral appears different colors when viewed from different angles. This is called **iridescence**.

Fluorescent Minerals: Check Out the Light Show!

Some minerals, such as calcite, can actually glow when you look at them under a special kind of light. These minerals are **fluorescent**, allowing them to absorb and change light so they appear a different color to the human eye. Tricky, huh?

QUIRKY QUARTZ

Quartz has proved itself to be very useful. It can be found just about anywhere—in watches, in electronics, in manufacturing, and even in jewelry. Some people wear it because they say it promotes healing.

QUARTZ—the most abundant mineral found at Earth's surface

Would You Like to See Your Future?

Cartoons sometimes show mediums looking into crystal balls so they can predict the future. Some people actually believe they can tell the future by looking into crystal balls. Such balls are made of clear quartz. Psychic Jeane Dixon used a crystal ball to predict that a man named Nikolai Bulganin would become a leader of the Soviet Union. Two years later, Dixon's prediction came true—or was it just a coincidence?

STRANGE-BUT-TRUE STORIES

DASHING DOLOMITE

For decades, scientists were stumped by the rocks and boulders that seemed to sail across Racetrack Playa, a plain in Death Valley National Park. Made of the mineral dolomite, the stones—some small enough to hold in your hands and others as large as a small child—leave trails like car tires, sometimes even traveling in curved tracks by pairs. The stones travel for just a few seconds or for as long as 16 minutes. How is this possible?

In 2014, scientists finally solved the mystery of the dashing dolomite. Covered in 3 in. (7 cm) of water, the playa would freeze overnight. As the sun rose, the cracking ice and wind sent the rocks sailing—and it was all caught on camera. But that doesn't make it any less amazing to see!

DOLOMITE— a mineral and a rock

ROCK-HARD FACT

Dolomite has a dual identity: It is a mineral but also a type of rock. Dolomite rocks are **sedimentary** rocks made mostly, but not entirely, of dolomite. (See pages 16–17 to learn about sedimentary rocks.)

11

To understand rocks is to understand our Earth and its history. That's because our planet's surface—called the crust—is made of layers of rocks. These layers are called **strata.** Beneath the crust is **magma,** a layer of **molten** rocks. At the center of Earth is a core made of solid minerals.

ROCK-HARD FACT

By studying strata and **fossils,** scientists can learn about the changes Earth has undergone throughout its history. Who needs a time machine?

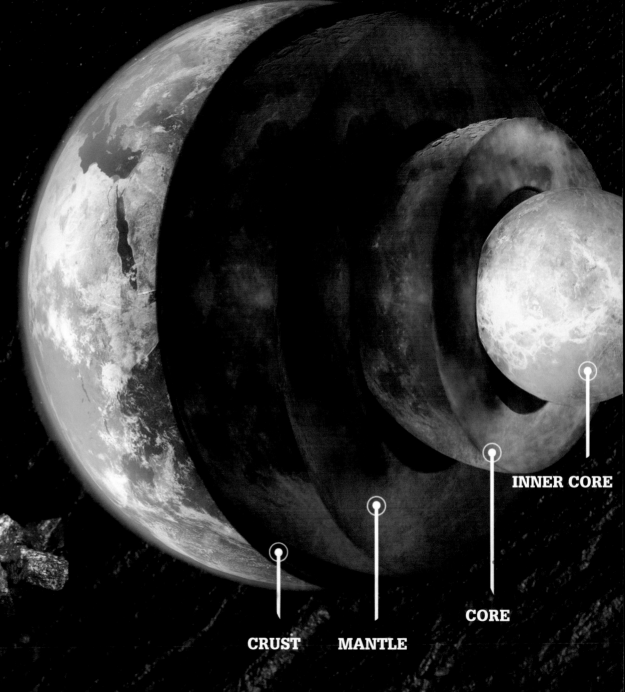

INNER CORE

CORE

CRUST   MANTLE

ROCKS

Types of Rocks

Rocks belong to one of three groups: **igneous**, **metamorphic**, and sedimentary. Natural processes, such as heat and pressure, sometimes change one type of rock to another—and sometimes even change them back again. In fact, the cycle of rock formation and change—further affected by **erosion**—never, ever stops.

IGNEOUS	SEDIMENTARY	METAMORPHIC
Granite	Sandstone	Gneiss
Pumice	Shale	Marble
Basalt	Flint	

EARTH'S STRATA
Earth's crust is between 3 to 45 mi. (5 to 70 km) thick. That's an awful lot of rock!

When molten rock becomes solid, it produces igneous rock. When molten material cools slowly inside the earth, it creates **intrusive** rocks. Sometimes magma within the earth escapes through cracks or **volcanos.** The magma pours out as **lava**, which cools into rock. Rocks that form like this are called **extrusive.**

RHYOLITE

OBSIDIAN

SNOWFLAKE
OBSIDIAN

PERIDOTITE

IGNEOUS ROCKS

IT'S EVERYWHERE!

Igneous rock is the most common rock type. It covers approximately 95 percent of Earth's upper crust, and there are more than 700 different types of igneous rock.

GABBRO

SCORIA

FIRE OPAL

FIRE OPAL

PEGMATITE

WELDED TUFF

15

You can usually spot sedimentary rocks by their layers. Sometimes these rocks appear to be glued together by cement. They are the second most common kind of rock. Over time and under pressure, bits of sediment in the form of dirt, rock, sand, or even living things become pressed down to become rock. Sedimentary rocks can be **organic**—meaning they contain parts of living things—or **inorganic**.

CONGLOMERATE

GYPSUM

LIMESTONE

OIL SHALE

CALCAREOUS TUFA

SEDIMENTARY ROCKS

IRON ORE

ALABASTER

SILTSTONE

DOLOMITE

A Day at the Beach

The sand beneath your feet as you walk along the beach comes from rocks that have been weathered and broken down—as in, really broken down!—over time.

COAL

Metamorphic rocks can be identified by the twists, swirls, and folds within them. These morphing, or changing, rocks begin as sedimentary and igneous rocks and are transformed over time by heat and pressure.

SCHIST

UNAKITE

PHYLLITE

SOAPSTONE

LAPIS LAZULI

METAMORPHIC ROCKS

SERPENTINE

Erosion at Its Coolest

Did you ever wonder how caves are formed? They're the result of erosion as rainwater—combined with carbon dioxide to create an acid—travels through soil and slowly dissolves limestone.

AMPHIBOLITE

HORNFELS

If you study rocks long enough, you eventually will be able to tell if a rock is igneous, sedimentary, or metamorphic. But that may be only part of any rock's story.

A rock that begins as igneous eventually may be exposed on the surface and eroded into **sediment** beds, where time and pressure create sedimentary rock. Over time, that same rock can be broken down and re-formed over and over again.

Sedimentary rock can also find its way beneath the surface, where heat and pressure will change it into something new—this time a metamorphic rock. That metamorphic rock can be pushed up to the surface and become

sedimentary again, or it can find its way deeper into the earth, where it will melt and become magma and eventually become igneous again. This is the rock cycle, which is actually nature's way of recycling rocks.

DEPOSITION

THE ROCK CYCLE

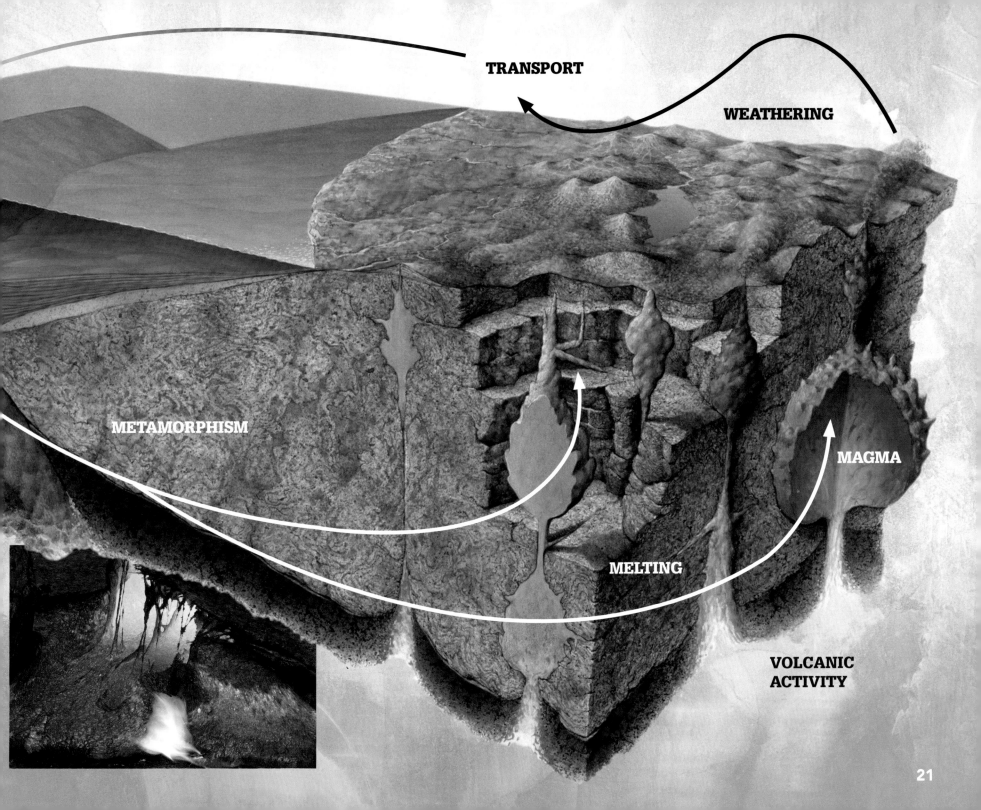

TRANSPORT

WEATHERING

METAMORPHISM

MELTING

MAGMA

VOLCANIC ACTIVITY

SHALE, THE FOSSIL-MAKER

In 2012, a top-secret park in Canada unearthed a treasure trove of fossilized finds: more than 3,000 ancient **specimens** that spanned 55 **species**, 12 of which were new to scientists. In the fossils, scientists could see hearts, livers, eyeballs, and even what the animals last ate!

How did so many fossils end up so perfectly preserved in one place? Scientists think the animals were buried in a mudslide so deeply that nothing—not even air—could reach them. The mud hardened into a type of sedimentary rock called shale, creating a time machine of sorts for scientists trying to understand Earth's history.

STRANGE-BUT-TRUE STORIES

ROCK-HARD FACT

Shale, the most common type of sedimentary rock, is formed when mud hardens. It may contain bits of minerals, such as quartz and calcite. It is usually gray and is a perfect choice for when you want to skip stones across a lake, river, or creek.

23

DIABASE, THE MUSIC-MAKER

Most people didn't attend rock concerts until the 1960s. But way back in 1890, visitors to the Pennsylvania countryside enjoyed what might have been the very first rock concert—played on real rocks! Dr. John J. Ott, joined by a brass band, struck a hammer to several pieces of rock, each of which played a different musical note.

The rocks were chunks of a type of igneous rock called diabase found at Ringing Rocks Park, where one of every three rocks can play a note when struck. The sound results in the same way as when a guitar string is plucked or a piano key is pressed. Because each rock plays a different note, Dr. Ott had to search long and hard through a boulder field to find the perfect members of his rock band. Today, musicians sometimes meet at Ringing Rocks Park for jam sessions.

DIABASE, also known as dolerite

Boulder field at Ringing Rocks Park

STRANGE-BUT-TRUE STORIES

24

Knock Them Out of the Park!

You have to strike them with a hammer to get a good sound.

25

Geodes—from a Latin word meaning "earthy"—are among nature's special treasures. They form from different kinds of minerals, so they're found in a rainbow of colors. Some contain crystals made of gemstones, such as amethyst or agate. Their unremarkable, "earthy" exteriors can distract you from the very remarkable treasures you find inside.

Cave of Crystals

In 2000, two brothers who worked in the Mexican mining industry discovered a limestone cave now known as the Cave of Crystals, a place as deadly hot as it is beautiful.

GEODES

MAKE YOUR OWN GEODES

Why search for a geode when you can make one of your own? All you'll need is a few common household items and an adult to help you.

WHAT YOU NEED

1. The clean shell halves of one egg
2. An egg carton
3. 2 cups of warm water in a bowl
4. Epsom salts
5. Food coloring

WHAT YOU DO

1. Set the eggshell halves in the carton, open ends up.
2. Stir Epsom salts into your bowl of warm water until the salts dissolve.
3. Add a few drops of food coloring, depending upon what color geode you want. Ask an adult to help you combine colors if you want to make purple, green, or orange. Or create your own color combination!
4. Gently and carefully pour your salty water into the eggshell halves.
5. Let the shells sit for a few days while you wait for the water to evaporate.
6. After a few days, your eggshells will be full of crystals!

1.

2.

3.

4.

5.

6.

GEODES: ENTOMBED AMPHIBIANS

Most people are pleasantly surprised by what they find inside a geode—but not everyone, especially if you don't like surprises of the bumpy or slimy variety. Sometimes a rock hound will open a geode to find a *living* frog or toad in a pile of mucus (aka snot). The animal will come to life for a few minutes before turning an unattractive gray color and dying.

How do frogs and toads survive inside geodes? One theory is that they are able to slow down their breathing, heart rates, and other bodily functions enough to survive, even over the thousands of years it could take for a rock to form around them.

ROCK-HARD FACT

Living amphibians have also been found inside pockets of coal, which, like geodes, forms slowly over time and under pressure.

STRANGE-BUT-TRUE STORIES

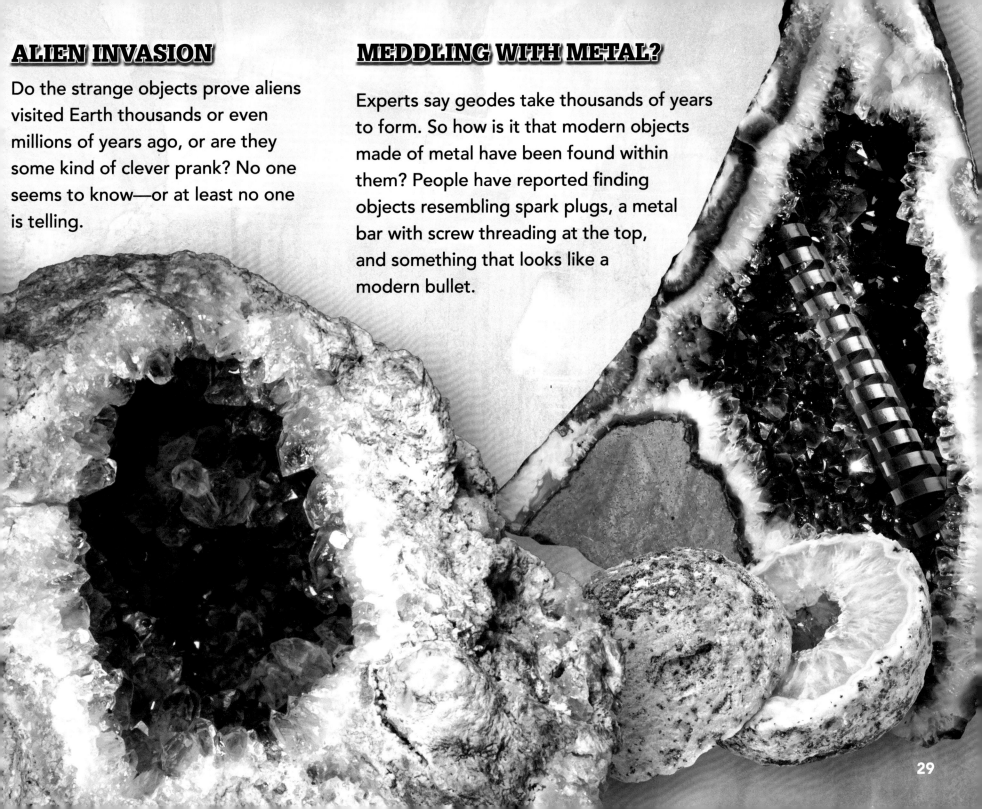

ALIEN INVASION

Do the strange objects prove aliens visited Earth thousands or even millions of years ago, or are they some kind of clever prank? No one seems to know—or at least no one is telling.

MEDDLING WITH METAL?

Experts say geodes take thousands of years to form. So how is it that modern objects made of metal have been found within them? People have reported finding objects resembling spark plugs, a metal bar with screw threading at the top, and something that looks like a modern bullet.

Of all the beautiful crystals formed by minerals, gems take the top prize. Gems are minerals that have been cut and polished to enhance their beauty. Used in jewelry (think of a diamond ring), gems increase in value based upon rarity. Diamonds, rubies, sapphires, and emeralds are among the most popular gems.

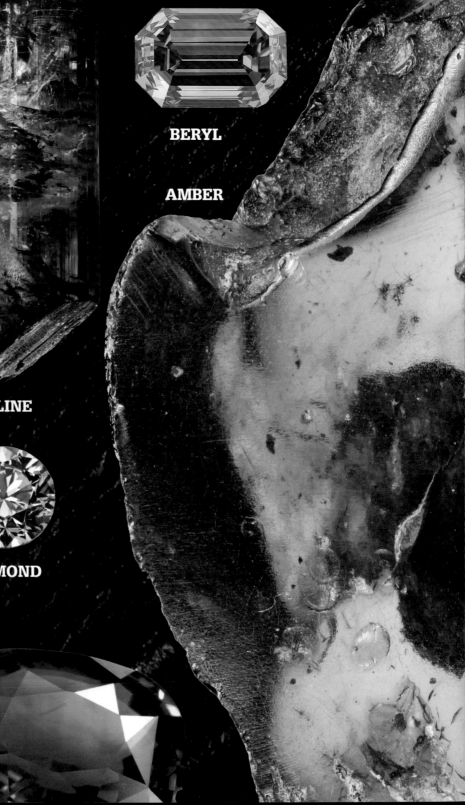

BERYL

AMBER

TOURMALINE

TOPAZ

ROSE
QUARTZ

DIAMOND

GARNET

OPAL

GEMS

SAPPHIRE

ROUGH RUBY

PEARL

PERIDOT

HIDDEN BEAUTY

Uncut and unpolished—or what some call "rough"—gemstones may not look like anything special. But in the hands of an expert, that boring stone becomes a precious treasure.

ROUGH SAPPHIRE

ROUGH GARNET

EMERALD

WHAT IS YOUR BIRTHSTONE?

Birthstones are gemstones that are associated with months of birth. Can you spot your birthstone?

JANUARY	FEBRUARY	MARCH
GARNET	AMETHYST	AQUAMARINE

APRIL	MAY	JUNE
DIAMOND	EMERALD	PEARL

JULY	AUGUST	SEPTEMBER
RUBY	PERIDOT	SAPPHIRE

OCTOBER	NOVEMBER	DECEMBER
TOURMALINE	CITRINE	BLUE TOPAZ

ROCK-HARD FACT

Gemstones are classified by their physical properties, like those listed on page 5.

Less than 100 of the more than 4,000 minerals found on Earth are worthy to be called gems. Precious gems are as fascinating as they are beautiful. Let's learn what makes these colorful stones so interesting, valuable, and maybe even deadly!

THE TOP TEN MOST EXPENSIVE DIAMONDS IN THE WORLD

1. **The Koh-I-Noor Diamond**, clear diamond, 105 carats, price: PRICELESS
2. **The Sancy Diamond**, pale yellow diamond, 55.23 carats, price: PRICELESS
3. **The Cullinan Diamond**, clear diamond, 3,106.75 carats, price: $2 billion
4. **The Hope Diamond**, blue diamond, 45.52 carats, price: $200–250 million
5. **The De Beers Centenary Diamond**, clear diamond, 273.85 carats, price: $100 million
6. **The Steinmetz Pink Diamond**, vivid pink diamond, 59.6 carats, price: $83 million
7. **The Wittelsbach Diamond**, blue diamond, 35.36 carats, price: $24.3 million
8. **The Heart of Eternity Diamond**, vivid blue diamond, 27.64 carats, price: $16 million
9. **The Moussaieff Red Diamond**, red diamond, 5.11 carats, price: $8 million
10. **The Allnatt Diamond**, vivid yellow diamond, 101.29 carats, price: $3 million

Inside a Diamond Mine
Diamond mining, done within giant, man-made craters, can be deadly work.

ROCK-HARD FACT

Gemstones are measured in carats (pronounced like *carrots*, the vegetable your mom may make you eat). One carat weighs 0.2 grams—just a fraction of an ounce!

A TREASURE TROVE OF PRECIOUS GEMS

The Curse of the Hope Diamond

Stories dating back to 1653 tell of terrible fates—murders, accidents, and beheadings—meeting the many owners of the diamond, but these stories are believed to have been attempts to increase the blue diamond's value. The stone has been on display—quite safely—at the Smithsonian National Museum of Natural History in Washington, DC, since 1958.

A Cure for Seasickness

Because of its healing properties, sailors once wore around their necks aquamarine gems as a cure for seasickness. They also believed the stone could protect them from shipwrecks.

CRYSTAL SYSTEMS

If you like minerals and gems, prepare to like geometry! Here are six geometric shapes of crystals.

CUBIC
Example: Halite

TETRAGONAL
Example: Zircon

HEXAGONAL
Example: Quartz

ORTHORHOMBIC
Example: Staurolite

MONOCLINIC
Example: Mica

TRICLINIC
Example: Cleavelandite

RUBIES

The ruby has proven to be one out-of-this-world gem. In 1969, scientists at the Lick Observatory in California succeeded in using rubies to bounce a laser beam off the moon—a beam 100,000 times as bright as the sun.

A core of rubies helped power the laser, which shoots a thin but powerful beam that holds together even across space. The laser helped scientists understand more about the moon and will, in turn, help them understand more about other moons and planets.

ROCK-HARD FACT

The first laser beam, also ruby-powered, was successfully tested in 1960. Modern lasers use many other minerals besides rubies. Different minerals produce different types of laser beams.

Old NASA moon rover uses ruby-powered lasers

STRANGE-BUT-TRUE STORIES

FLUORITE

Since 1982, when deposits of the glowing fluorite were found in a mine in China, craftsmen have been able to use fluorite to create jewelry and other decorative items. They were even able to use glow-in-the-dark fluorite to recreate a nearly 600 year-old priceless, glow-in-the-dark pearl the size of a beach ball that was stolen from the palace of a Chinese prince.

Bright as the Moon

The fluorite ball on display at the palace glows all night long, changing from green to white and back again. "It is as beautiful and bright as the moon," one official said glowingly.

ROCK-HARD FACT

Many types of fluorite are fluorescent and will glow when under an ultraviolet light. Other types don't glow, but they are still pretty.

35

Rocks have so much to teach us that we could spend a lifetime—even many lifetimes—unearthing their secrets. Some people spend their entire lives studying the resources, history, stability, and power contained within the rocks beneath us. Let's meet a few of them!

PALEONTOLOGIST

A **paleontologist** studies fossilized animals and plants, from living things so tiny they can only be seen under a microscope to creatures so large (like a T. rex) they're terrifying!

GEOLOGIST

Geologists study materials within the earth and the history they reveal, as well as events such as landslides, volcanoes, floods, and earthquakes.

SO YOU WANT TO BE A ROCK STAR

ENGINEERING GEOLOGIST

An expert in rock strength and soil composition, an engineering geologist works with other professionals to build bridges, roads, dams, and tunnels. The job can be risky but is seldom boring!

FIELD GEOLOGIST

Have you ever looked at a map? That's the work of a field geologist, who also looks at geological activity and monitors the **environment**.

The Wave, Coconino County, Arizona

VOLCANOLOGIST

A **volcanologist** studies the formation, eruption, and history of volcanoes. These scientists must really *lava* their work!

SEDIMENTOLOGISTS

A **sedimentologist** studies sedimentary rocks, which cover 75 percent of Earth's surface, to understand geological history. Such rocks contain our fossil records.

Natural rock formations in a cave system in Eastern Australia

STRATIGRAPHER

A **stratigrapher** studies strata, whether volcanic or sedimentary, and what those strata tell us about Earth's history.

GEOPHYSICIST

A **geophysicist** uses gravity, magnetic, electrical, and **seismic** methods to study the earth, sometimes to find oil or valuable minerals and sometimes to make sure areas are safe for construction.

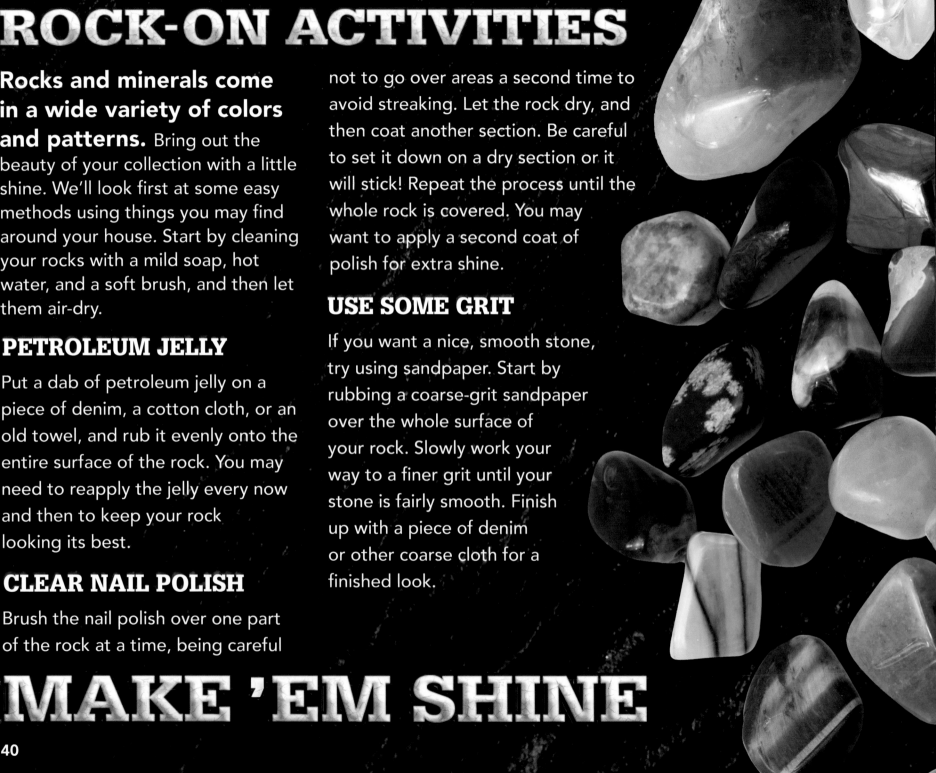

ROCK-ON ACTIVITIES

Rocks and minerals come in a wide variety of colors and patterns. Bring out the beauty of your collection with a little shine. We'll look first at some easy methods using things you may find around your house. Start by cleaning your rocks with a mild soap, hot water, and a soft brush, and then let them air-dry.

PETROLEUM JELLY

Put a dab of petroleum jelly on a piece of denim, a cotton cloth, or an old towel, and rub it evenly onto the entire surface of the rock. You may need to reapply the jelly every now and then to keep your rock looking its best.

CLEAR NAIL POLISH

Brush the nail polish over one part of the rock at a time, being careful not to go over areas a second time to avoid streaking. Let the rock dry, and then coat another section. Be careful to set it down on a dry section or it will stick! Repeat the process until the whole rock is covered. You may want to apply a second coat of polish for extra shine.

USE SOME GRIT

If you want a nice, smooth stone, try using sandpaper. Start by rubbing a coarse-grit sandpaper over the whole surface of your rock. Slowly work your way to a finer grit until your stone is fairly smooth. Finish up with a piece of denim or other coarse cloth for a finished look.

MAKE 'EM SHINE

MAKE YOUR OWN ROCK TUMBLER

A rock tumbler is another way to get really smooth stones. Are you ready to shake things up? Start by choosing similar-sized pebbles of a similar hardness. (See page 5 to help determine hardness.) Pick rocks with colors and patterns that you like. Try rubbing some water onto your rocks to see their colors.

WHAT YOU NEED

1. A large plastic jar with a screw-on lid

2. Coarse sand

3. Medium-grit sand

4. Fine-grit sand

5. A selection of pebbles

6. Water

WHAT YOU DO

1. Put your rocks into the plastic jar, and add enough coarse sand to cover the rocks.

2. Fill the jar about a third of the way with water to make a gritty slurry.

3. Any time you find yourself just sitting—while you're watching TV or just hanging out with friends—take some time to shake and roll your jar. Warning: It's going to be noisy!

4. After a week, check your rocks' progress. If they look less rough, replace the sand with a medium-grit sand, add more water to the jar, and start the process over again.

5. Check your rocks after another week. If they are smoothing up nicely, change to a fine-grit sand, and continue shaking and rolling the jar daily until your rocks have the smoothness you want.

6. Rub some mineral oil into your polished stones using a piece of denim or an old towel. Don't wash them, or they'll lose their shine!

No matter how hard they are, rocks don't last forever. They can undergo change in many ways. This change is called weathering.

BIOLOGICAL WEATHERING

You have already learned about how erosion—the product of wind, water, and ice—wears away at rocks over time. Rocks can also experience **biological** weathering. Tree roots can crack rocks, and slow-growing plants, such as lichen, can break down rocks and even change their composition.

CHEMICAL WEATHERING

Another way rocks undergo change is by chemical weathering. Water, acids, and gases slowly dissolve or react with minerals in the rock and create new compounds. Would you like to try to recreate this process? Take a look at the instructions on the next page.

DO-IT-YOURSELF ROCK WEATHERING

You can be a rock's agent of change using a couple of ingredients found in most kitchens. Keep in mind that lemon juice and vinegar are weak acids. Get your parent's permission before using them.

WHAT YOU DO

1. Put a few drops of lemon juice on one rock.

2. Put a few drops of vinegar on the second rock.

3. Listen carefully!

WHAT HAPPENS NEXT?

Lemon juice and vinegar contain acetic acid, which dissolves calcium carbonate. If you heard fizzing when you dripped the lemon juice or vinegar on a limestone, chalk, or calcite sample, you did the experiment right! But quartz, which doesn't contain any calcium carbonate, will not react to these acids.

You have learned how to test for calcium carbonate in rocks and minerals. Now it's time to dig deep so you can learn even more about your rocks. Choose a few different types of rocks from your collection, or look around your home or school for some samples if you haven't started a collection. Make sure you get your parents' permission before doing these tests.

1. MAGNETISM

Touch a strong magnet to your rock. Is the magnet drawn to the rock? If so, your rock contains the mineral iron.

2. FLOATING

Fill a plastic cup or jar with water, and drop your rock in it. If it floats, you have a **porous** igneous rock known as pumice.

3. HARDNESS

Try scratching your rock with your fingernail. If it scratches, your rock is very soft according to the Mohs' scale of hardness.

Now try scratching your rock with another rock. Did it leave a mark? What happens when you scratch the second rock with the first one? The one that leaves a scratch mark is the hardest rock.

PUT YOUR ROCKS TO THE TEST

4. STREAK TEST

Have a parent help you find a loose white bathroom or kitchen tile. Then rub your rock across the unglazed side of tile. You can also use the bottom of a white ceramic coffee mug. What color is the streak? Sometimes the streak color matches the rock color, and sometimes it doesn't. The rock's streak color is considered its true color.

5. LUSTER

You've learned ways to make your rocks shine, but some rocks have a glow all their own. Wash your rock with water, and let it air-dry. Is it shiny? If so, it has luster. Compare the luster of your rocks. What other traits do the shiny ones have in common? What else do you notice about the dull ones?

Deadly Rocks!

In 2013, neighbors in a Florida community awoke to a deafening noise and a terrified scream from the back bedroom. A house was swallowed up by the earth as a man slept inside! The house continued to sink into the pit until all hope of saving the man was lost. So what on earth—or under the earth—happened? Florida rests on a bed of limestone, which dissolves over time as the rock absorbs water like a sponge. The limestone caves in when it can no longer hold the weight on top of it. That rock would definitely fail the hardness test!

ATOM
the smallest unit of matter

BIOLOGICAL
relating to living things

COMPOSITION
how or of what something is made

ELECTROMAGNETIC
relating to electric and
magnetic fields

ENVIRONMENT
the area or conditions in which a
person, plant, or animal lives

EROSION
the process in which wind, water,
and ice wear away rock over time

EVAPORATE
to turn from liquid into gas
or vapor

EXTRUSIVE
forming on Earth's surfaces

FLUORESCENT
absorbing light of one color and
reflecting another, giving it the
appearance of glowing

FOSSIL
an impression of an ancient living
thing left in rock

GEODE
a crystal-filled cavity, or hole,
inside a rock

GEOLOGIST
an expert in the study of Earth's
makeup and physical history

GEOPHYSICIST
someone who uses gravity,
magnetic, electrical, and seismic
methods to study Earth

IGNEOUS
rock formed from cooled magma
or lava

INORGANIC
not coming from living things

INTRUSIVE
forming within the Earth

IRIDESCENCE
the ability to show different colors
when viewed from different angles
or using different lights

LAVA
molten rock

MAGMA
hot liquid found beneath
Earth's crust

MAGNETORECEPTION
the ability to find direction using
Earth's magnetic field

GLOSSARY

METAMORPHIC
rock formed by heat and pressure from sedimentary and igneous rock

MINERAL
a hard material from which rocks and gems are made that is found in nature and is not made of living things

MOLTEN
made liquid by heat

ORGANIC
coming from living things

PALEONTOLOGIST
a scientist who studies the fossils of plants and animals

POROUS
full of holes through which water or air can pass

SEDIMENT
particles of organic or inorganic matter carried by wind or rain and deposited on land or at the bottom of a body of water

SEDIMENTARY
made from sediment deposited by wind or water

SEDIMENTOLOGIST
a scientist who studies sedimentary rocks to learn about Earth's physical history

SEISMIC
relating to vibrations in Earth's crust, sometimes produced by natural events, such as earthquakes, and sometimes by man-made explosions

SPECIES
a group of similar living things

SPECIMEN
a typical example of something of a particular type or kind

STRATA
layers of rock in the ground

STRATIGRAPHER
an expert in strata and their order in terms of Earth's geological history

UNIFORM
the same throughout

VOLCANO
a mountain or hill from which hot gas or vapor, rocks, and lava erupt from deep within the earth

VOLCANOLOGIST
an expert in the study of the formation and eruption patterns of volcanoes